THE LEADERSHIP PIN CODE

UNLOCKING THE KEY TO WILLING AND WINNING RELATIONSHIPS

THE ABC WORKBOOK

DR. NASHATER DEU SOLHEIM

COPYRIGHT ©2021 NASHATER DEU SOLHEIM
All rights reserved.

THE LEADERSHIP PIN CODE: THE ABC WORKBOOK
Unlocking the Key to Willing and Winning Relationships

ISBN 978-1-5445-2319-4

Welcome to your personal

PIN CODE
WORKBOOK!

This is your toolkit to
accompany the text book

Let's begin!

The Leadership PIN code ABC framework gets better with practise. Each time you plan your approach, behaviour and conversation, receive feedback and adapt, the further towards engaged you'll go.

When you use this workbook, pro-flect on what are you going to do now. What action will you take to move the needle towards engaged? What are you planning to say to that person you're about to meet or the room you're about to walk into?

Check your body language as you close the book and walk toward the door. Think about what you're actually going to say next.

Take a minute right now: what's in your PIN code for the encounter you're about to have?

Keep engaging!

The PIN Code is about finding the hook—the interest and motivation—of the other person for creating a willing and winning relationship that delivers the results the business needs with you in the lead.

PERSUADE, INFLUENCE, NEGOTIATE = PIN

Your PIN Code is how you take what you know about your business and your mandate and get to that point where you are truly inspiring others and fostering the culture your business needs.

PIN is the conduit, the connector and the bridge between your head and what you know and the reason for being in the role and responsibility.

I've developed a simple but impactful, common sense, easy-to-use method that exercises the PIN muscles, an ABC method of approach (A) behaviour (B) and conversation (C) that, once tried, leaves a memorable impact.

If PIN is what you want to do, ABC is how you do it.

Approach / Advanced Preparation

Your mindset, your research into people, context, how you prepare for individual encounters or meetings by taking the time to learn about their interests, culture, or goals.

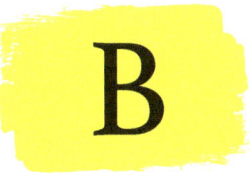

Behaviour / Body Language

The physical behaviour and manner you use when meeting with people, including body language, choosing the right arena for the encounter, and how you set up a room or manage virtual meetings.

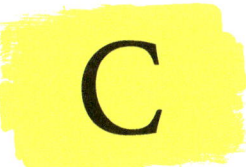

Conversation

The questions you ask, responses you give, and how you steer the conversation and dialogue, managing resistance and conflict, building trust.

Approach / Advanced Preparation

Behaviour / Body Language

Conversation

HOW TO USE THIS WORKBOOK

Create a Strategy

Create an ABC plan for each meeting or event:

1. Use the ABC individual sheets—"Dig Deeper Workpage"—to write down and brainstorm each of the A, B and C tools you want to use for your intended purpose—whether that is a meeting, negotiation, or simple conversation.

2. Once you have brainstormed the A, B and C individually then you can summarise your overall strategy/plan for this meeting into the ABC "Dig in Cheatsheet" that follows the individual sheets. To make it even easier to use in your meeting, once completed, you can tear out the Cheatsheet page and take it with you into the meeting you have planned for.

3. If you need help remembering some of the tools you might use from the textbook—go to the section called "Tools Checklist" where you can find a list of those for A, B and C. A tip is to put the textbook page reference next to the tools so you can find them easily when you need them.

4. Use the facing "additional notes" page for memory jots like the names, titles, roles of the people you are meeting, or key facts of the business or simply to capture your own observations during the meeting. Record your favourite tools for A, B and C in the "My Favourites" section at the end of the book and include references to the text book or links to web-tools etc. for future reference and make a note of what these favourites are good for.

Tips: Use The Leadership PIN Code text book and relevant chapters for ideas, and add your own tools for each. Think back to times when you have had success before and write down what worked or think about someone you admire who has done this successfully and jot down what they did.

Dig Deep Workpage

A

Additional Notes

APPROACH / ADVANCED PREPARATION

Dig Deep Workpage

BEHAVIOUR / BODY LANGUAGE

B

Additional Notes

Dig Deep Workpage

C

Additional Notes

Dig In Cheatsheet

Purpose:

Date:

A APPROACH / ADVANCED PREPARATION
_____
_____
_____
_____
_____
_____
_____

B BEHAVIOUR / BODY LANGUAGE
_____
_____
_____
_____
_____
_____
_____

C CONVERSATION
_____
_____
_____
_____
_____
_____
_____

Dig In Cheatsheet

Purpose:

Date:

A   APPROACH / ADVANCED PREPARATION

B   BEHAVIOUR / BODY LANGUAGE

C   CONVERSATION

Dig Deep Workpage

A
Additional Notes

Dig Deep Workpage

B

Additional Notes

BEHAVIOUR / BODY LANGUAGE

Dig Deep Workpage

C

Additional Notes

Dig In Cheatsheet

Purpose:

Date:

A — APPROACH / ADVANCED PREPARATION

B — BEHAVIOUR / BODY LANGUAGE

C — CONVERSATION

Dig In Cheatsheet

Purpose:

Date:

A APPROACH / ADVANCED PREPARATION

_____

_____

_____

_____

_____

_____

_____

B BEHAVIOUR / BODY LANGUAGE

_____

_____

_____

_____

_____

_____

_____

C CONVERSATION

_____

_____

_____

_____

_____

_____

_____

Dig Deep Workpage

A *Additional Notes*

Dig Deep Workpage

B

Additional Notes

Dig Deep Workpage

C

Additional Notes

Dig In Cheatsheet

Purpose:

Date:

A — APPROACH / ADVANCED PREPARATION

_____
_____
_____
_____
_____
_____
_____
_____

B — BEHAVIOUR / BODY LANGUAGE

_____
_____
_____
_____
_____
_____
_____
_____

C — CONVERSATION

_____
_____
_____
_____
_____
_____
_____
_____

Dig In Cheatsheet

Purpose:

Date:

A APPROACH / ADVANCED PREPARATION
_____
_____
_____
_____
_____
_____
_____

B BEHAVIOUR / BODY LANGUAGE
_____
_____
_____
_____
_____
_____
_____

C CONVERSATION
_____
_____
_____
_____
_____
_____
_____

Dig Deep Workpage

A *Additional Notes*

Dig Deep Workpage

B
Additional Notes

BEHAVIOUR / BODY LANGUAGE

Dig Deep Workpage

C

Additional Notes

Dig In Cheatsheet

Purpose:

Date:

A APPROACH / ADVANCED PREPARATION

B BEHAVIOUR / BODY LANGUAGE

C CONVERSATION

Dig In Cheatsheet

Purpose:

Date:

A APPROACH / ADVANCED PREPARATION

B BEHAVIOUR / BODY LANGUAGE

C CONVERSATION

Dig Deep Workpage

A

Additional Notes

Dig Deep Workpage

Additional Notes

Dig Deep Workpage

C

Additional Notes

Dig In Cheatsheet

Purpose:

Date:

A — APPROACH / ADVANCED PREPARATION

_____
_____
_____
_____
_____
_____
_____

B — BEHAVIOUR / BODY LANGUAGE

_____
_____
_____
_____
_____
_____
_____

C — CONVERSATION

_____
_____
_____
_____
_____
_____
_____

Dig In Cheatsheet

Purpose:

Date:

A APPROACH / ADVANCED PREPARATION

_____

_____

_____

_____

_____

_____

B BEHAVIOUR / BODY LANGUAGE

_____

_____

_____

_____

_____

_____

C CONVERSATION

_____

_____

_____

_____

_____

_____

Dig Deep Workpage

A

Additional Notes

Dig Deep Workpage

B

Additional Notes

BEHAVIOUR / BODY LANGUAGE

Dig Deep Workpage

C

Additional Notes

Dig In Cheatsheet

Purpose:

Date:

A APPROACH / ADVANCED PREPARATION

B BEHAVIOUR / BODY LANGUAGE

C CONVERSATION

Dig In Cheatsheet

Purpose:

Date:

A APPROACH / ADVANCED PREPARATION

_____
_____
_____
_____
_____
_____
_____

B BEHAVIOUR / BODY LANGUAGE

_____
_____
_____
_____
_____
_____
_____

C CONVERSATION

_____
_____
_____
_____
_____
_____
_____

Dig Deep Workpage

A *Additional Notes*

Dig Deep Workpage

B

Additional Notes

Dig Deep Workpage

C

Additional Notes

Dig In Cheatsheet

Purpose:

Date:

A — APPROACH / ADVANCED PREPARATION

_____
_____
_____
_____
_____
_____
_____

B — BEHAVIOUR / BODY LANGUAGE

_____
_____
_____
_____
_____
_____
_____

C — CONVERSATION

_____
_____
_____
_____
_____
_____
_____

Dig In Cheatsheet

Purpose:

Date:

A — APPROACH / ADVANCED PREPARATION

B — BEHAVIOUR / BODY LANGUAGE

C — CONVERSATION

Advanced preparation isn't limited to *researching* the other person and practising your speech. The *mindset* you carry into a meeting will *leave its mark* on everyone in attendance

from THE LEADERSHIP PIN CODE
by Dr. Nashater Deu Solheim

TOOLS CHECKLIST

Approach / Advanced Preparation

Checklist:
- Consider their Values and Interests and Priorities
- Don't assume or judge - be curious
- Be aware of your own blind spots and biases and check them at the door. Remove assumptions.
- Be prepared for and invite the right people
- Prepare your mindset and avoid the funnel of gloom
- Approach it as a game of win-win, not a battle, and find common ground
- Adopt a positive attitude—doing the opposite behaviour if it helps
- Prepare for resistance
- Empathise with their interests
- Do your research
- Diligent planning

Tools:
- Stakeholders knowledge and mapping
- RACI tool
- TRUST model
- Fantasy and Visualization
- Rhetoric
- BATNA ,WATNA, ZOPA
- Anchoring
- Co-brainstorming
- Questioning
- Techniques

Be aware of inconsistencies between your *body language* and your *intent* or *words*, because those inconsistencies can mislead

from THE LEADERSHIP PIN CODE
by Dr. Nashater Deu Solheim

TOOLS CHECKLIST

Behaviour / Body Language

Checklist:
- Your body language
    - Open arms
    - Use your head
    - Eye contact
    - Mirroring
    - Opposite behaviour
    - Dress code

Check the Room:
- Set the room
    - 90 degrees vs 180 degrees
- Meeting arena and length
    - standing versus sitting or walk and talk
    - 45 minutes instead of an hour
- Hierarchy of virtual meetings:
    - video conferencing
    - phone
    - mail
    - text

Remember the platinum rule:
it's not about how you'd like to deliver
the message, but how the receiver
would like to hear the message.

from THE LEADERSHIP PIN CODE
by Dr. Nashater Deu Solheim

TOOLS CHECKLIST

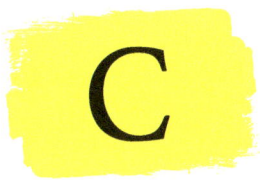

Conversation

Questioning Types (5 Cs):
1. **Curious:** to resolve conflict, disagreements, polarised ideas, resistance or opposition
2. **Circular:** to dig deeper, for example into values, motivations, drivers
3. **Confirming:** to ensure you've understood what was said, data is correct, showing empathy
4. **Clarifying:** to determine meaning and intention, exploring ideas, rationales
5. **Challenging/Investigative:** to test a situation or hypothesis, provoke opposing or new ideas, open up for pressure-testing existing ideas or concepts

Other:
- Knights Move
- NLP—Neuro Linguistic Programming : audio, visual, kinaesthetic
- Ladder of Inference—disagreements and conflicts
- Don't ask WHY of people
- 4 BUMS on a bench—Who What Where When How
- BUT out
- Socratic questioning
- Curious questioning
- Tone of voice
- Open sharing versus brutal honesty
- Language mirroring
- Feedback
- Silence and interruption
- Managing resistance and pushback
- Create rules of engagement

First impressions count,
but *influence* lasts longer.

from THE LEADERSHIP PIN CODE
by Dr. Nashater Deu Solheim

My Favourite ABCs

Tools	Useful For

My Favourite ABCs

Tools	Useful For

C

My Favourite ABCs

Tools	Useful For

The best way to practise the *ABC* is to try it out in a short encounter.

from **THE LEADERSHIP PIN CODE**
by **Dr. Nashater Deu Solheim**

THE LEADERSHIP PIN CODE

UNLOCKING THE KEY TO WILLING AND WINNING RELATIONSHIPS

#1 Amazon Bestseller
and recommended by
Forbes *and* Harvard Business Review

To learn more about working with Dr. Nashater Deu Solheim directly or attending one of her courses please check her homepage:

www.nashaterdeusolheim.com

Buy the book on most online bookstores, including Amazon.

An engaged leader who's been a leader for 5 years can be far more effective than an entitled leader who continues to lead for 35 years in the same ineffective way as when she started.

from **THE LEADERSHIP PIN CODE**
by Dr. Nashater Deu Solheim

About the Author

Dr Nashater Deu Solheim is CEO of Progressing Minds and author of *The Leadership PIN Code: Unlocking the Key to Willing and Winning Relationships*, which debuted on the 2020 Forbes list of 8 books "...that will make you reconsider how you manage relationships". She is an HBR contributor, executive coach on leadership influence, and a keynote speaker on her experience as a psychologist working with psychopaths, the serving military and with leaders in business settings. She is an accomplished moderator on the international stage. Nashater has over 25 years of practical business experience across diverse sectors for governments, global corporate, SMEs and with entrepreneurs. Nashater has held executive leadership positions within strategy, and leadership development in international corporations and SMEs. She holds a doctorate in Psychology from the UK and trained as an Expert Negotiator at Harvard Law School.

For More Information

If you're interested in PIN® coaching and training programs or becoming a PIN® Leadership Consultant or Training Partner and having access to our unique expertise and tools for your own organisations or clients of all sizes, in all industries, please send your enquiry to *post@progressingminds.com*.

www.ingramcontent.com/pod-product-compliance
Lightning Source LLC
LaVergne TN
LVHW081525060526
838200LV00044B/2000